# MONARCH BUTTERFLIES

## Life Cycles

**ABDO**
Publishing Company

A Buddy Book
by **Julie Murray**

## VISIT US AT
**www.abdopublishing.com**

Published by ABDO Publishing Company, 4940 Viking Drive, Edina, Minnesota 55435.

Copyright © 2007 by Abdo Consulting Group, Inc. International copyrights reserved in all countries. No part of this book may be reproduced in any form without written permission from the publisher. Buddy Books™ is a trademark and logo of ABDO Publishing Company.

Printed in the United States.

Coordinating Series Editor: Sarah Tieck
Contributing Editor: Michael P. Goecke
Graphic Design: Deb Coldiron
Cover Photograph: Photos.com
Interior Photographs/Illustrations: Animals Animals/Earth Scenes, Fotosearch, Media Bakery, Photos.com

## Library of Congress Cataloging-in-Publication Data

Murray, Julie, 1969–
    Monarch butterflies / Julie Murray.
        p. cm. — (Life cycles)
    ISBN-13:  978-1-59928-708-9
    ISBN-10:  1-59928-708-0
    1. Monarch butterfly—Juvenile literature.  I. Title.

QL561.D3M87 2007
595.78'9—dc22
                                                                2006031437

# Table Of Contents

# What Is A Life Cycle?

Monarch butterflies are living things. The world is made up of many kinds of life. People are alive. So are blue jays, grasshoppers, lions, and roses.

A monarch butterfly.

Every living thing has a life cycle. A life cycle is made up of many changes and processes. During a life cycle, living things are born, they grow, and they reproduce. And eventually, they die. Different living things start life and grow up in unique ways.

What do you know about the life cycle of a monarch butterfly?

# Meet The Monarch Butterfly

There are more than 15,000 different species of butterfly. The monarch butterfly is one of those species.

A monarch's body is similar to that of other butterflies.

Monarchs migrate across North America. They spend different parts of their lives in different places. Monarchs spend winters in warm places, such as California and Mexico. During the summers, they migrate to northern places, such as Canada.

Monarchs reproduce in areas where milkweed plants grow. The caterpillar eats milkweed.

# A Monarch's Life

A monarch's life cycle has four main stages. Its life begins as an egg.

A monarch egg.

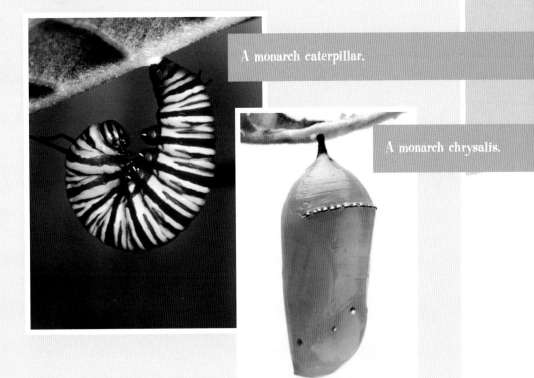

A monarch caterpillar.

A monarch chrysalis.

When the egg hatches, the monarch is born as a caterpillar, or larva. This caterpillar grows a hard shell called a chrysalis, or pupa.

The chrysalis then goes through a **process** of change called metamorphosis. During this time, the butterfly is forming inside the chrysalis.

When the monarch crawls out of the chrysalis, it is an adult butterfly. This is the last stage of a monarch's life. As a butterfly, a monarch ages, and eventually dies.

A monarch butterfly emerges from a chrysalis.

# Guess What?

Antennae

…Monarch butterflies have six legs and a pair of antennae. The antennae help butterflies smell and keep their balance.

…A monarch butterfly's orange and black wings get their bright colors and pattern from thousands of tiny scales.

Scales on a monarch's wing.

…Monarch and viceroy butterflies look like twins! This helps keep the viceroy safe from predators. Why? Because monarchs taste bad to hungry predators.

How can you tell monarchs and viceroys apart? They have similar wing patterns. But, the viceroy has a black stripe on its bottom wings. Monarchs do not have this.

Viceroy

13

# Starting To Grow

During the reproductive part of the monarch's life cycle, females mate with males. After this, the females lay sticky eggs on milkweed plants. They can quickly lay many eggs.

A newborn caterpillar is also called a larva.

The eggs take a few days to hatch. When an egg hatches, a caterpillar comes out and immediately begins eating.

Monarch caterpillars eat only milkweed. This helps keep them safe from many predators. This is because milkweed is poisonous to many other animals.

A newborn caterpillar begins eating milkweed right away.

# From Caterpillar To Butterfly

When they become too big for their skin, caterpillars molt. Growing caterpillars shed their skin, or molt, five times.

After about four weeks, a caterpillar is fully grown. Then, it stops eating and sheds its skin one last time. In place of new skin, the caterpillar grows a hard covering and turns into a chrysalis, or pupa.

When the chrysalis forms, metamorphosis has started.

The chrysalis then goes through a process called metamorphosis. Metamorphosis takes a couple of weeks. During this time, the chrysalis changes into a butterfly!

# Life As An Adult

When a butterfly first crawls out of the chrysalis, its wings are wet and wrinkled. But in a short time, the butterfly is flying through the air!

A monarch butterfly spends much of its life looking for food. Monarch butterflies love to feed on flowers. Using its proboscis, the monarch sucks sweet nectar from flowers.

Each autumn, monarchs migrate. They travel from cool places to warm locations. Some fly all the way from Canada to Mexico. Monarch butterflies can fly 80 miles (129 km) in one day!

Monarchs gather in warm places during the cold winter months.

# Endings And Beginnings

Adult monarch butterflies have different life spans. Usually, a monarch dies when its body gets old. Death is the end of one monarch butterfly's life. But, it is not the end of the species.

Most adult butterflies live from two to six weeks.

Because monarchs can reproduce, their species continues on. When a caterpillar hatches from an egg, it adds to a new generation of butterflies. This is the beginning of a new life cycle.

# Can You Guess?

**Q:** If your job was studying butterflies, what would you be called?
**A:** A lepidopterist.

**Q:** Migrating butterflies live longest. How long can some of these butterflies survive?
**A:** Six months or longer!

Monarchs that hatch in the fall and migrate can live for many months.

# Important Words

**generation**  a group that is living at the same time and is about the same age.

**mate**  to engage in an act that leads to reproduction.

**nectar**  a sweet liquid, or sugar water, that flowering plants make.

**predator**  an animal that hunts and eats other animals.

**proboscis**  the tubelike mouthpart that a butterfly uses for feeding.

**process**  a way of doing something.

**reproduce**  to produce offspring, or children.

**species**  living things that are very much alike.

**unique**  different.

## Web Sites

To learn more about monarch butterflies, visit ABDO Publishing Company on the World Wide Web. Web site links about monarch butterflies are featured on our Book Links page. These links are routinely monitored and updated to provide the most current information available.

**www.abdopublishing.com**

# Index